Breaking Free...
from the spirit of death

Jonathan Hunter
Guidebook Edition

The thief comes only to steal and kill and destroy; I have come that they may have life, and have it to the full.

John 10:10

Acknowledgments

—∽∾∽—

I would like to express my heartfelt thanks to the Embracing Life family around the world who have given their prayers, love and time so that the Body of Christ may know and experience His abundant life. At the top of the list are Neil and Debbie Driscoll who embody the heart of Embracing life Ministries—encouraging people in every context to live life to the full. Special thanks to Marilyn Evenstad for the initial inspiration for this *Guidebook*, and also to the first More Life! Team: Nancy Lang, Gary and Karen Greeno (with the Driscolls). Their experience and wisdom is shared in these pages.

Table of Contents

—⌇⌇⌇—

Author's Introduction to *More Life!*

——∾∾∾——

You have made known to me the path of life... Psalm 16:11

This *Guidebook Edition* is adapted from the original *Breaking Free...from the spirit of death* booklet, first published in 2002 (available through Xulon press). Years of teaching and ministering all over the world has taught me that unknowing acceptance of the spirit of death is pandemic in the body of Christ. *More Life!* offers group members practical, spiritual tools to help them break free from death's influences through discussion, reflection, prayer, and journaling.

Essentially, *More Life!* is all about hope and possibility, overcoming thoughts of helplessness, hopelessness and worthlessness. It is about the good news that we can be partakers of the fullness of life that is our inheritance in Christ Jesus.

Though attendance through all eight sessions is optimal, when used in a drop-in (open) group format, it is suggested that you read the following paragraph as an introduction at the beginning of each meeting:

> More Life! *equips Christians to effectively identify and confront destructive influences*

in their lives. More Life! *groups encourage victorious living in the face of the varied manifestations of death. Even a "mountain" of sorrow and personal challenges can be removed with a "mustard seed" of faith through the Father's love, the resurrection life of Jesus Christ, and the Holy Spirit who indwells every Christian. It is this faith that we are teaching participants to activate and exercise on an ongoing basis. The result: one is liberated from dominating, detrimental influences and free for more abundant living in Christ.*

More Life! small groups may be presented in various formats: as a weekend intensive, e.g. Friday evening, all day Saturday; over two Saturday sessions; or as successive weekly meetings. The format is left up to the leader's discretion and preferences. We have added helpful notes for leaders in Appendix V.

Be sure and have enough *More Life!* booklets on hand for all participants to follow along with the teaching. An option for participants to buy the booklets is recommended. This allows group members time to read each session beforehand, enabling greater understanding and interaction. For information on seminars, trainings, and other healing opportunities or to purchase ELM publications (*Embracing Life Series, More Glory!, More Hope!, etc.*), including additional copies of *More Life!,* please visit: www.embracinglife.us or Xulon Press: www.xulonpress.com

Jonathan Hunter: My Personal Odyssey of Discovery

—*ชชช*—

Indeed, in our hearts we felt the sentence of death. But this happened that we might not rely on ourselves but on God, who raises the dead. 2 Cor. 1:9

In October of 1985, I tested positive for HIV, the AIDS virus. After three-and-a-half years of abstaining from sexual activity and drugs, this news came as quite a blow. Up until that time, I had naively believed that becoming a Christian automatically healed me of any damaging medical consequences from my previously promiscuous lifestyle. The counselor at the clinic informed me otherwise. "Nope," he said, "the virus is definitely there. You're infected alright."

I was shocked. I couldn't believe it. I numbly walked out to my car; my world now surreally turned upside-down. As I drove back to the office where friends were waiting, I cried out to God: "This is what I got saved for! What's so great about being born again... and infected! New creature in Christ? Big deal! You can't even get rid of a little virus! Where's the hope, the future? I'm dead meat now!" My whole body was burning from the emotional turmoil churning inside me. The thought of facing friends with the news made me feel sick.

NOT WHAT I EXPECTED

My life as a Christian—a mere five years—was in for a BIG growth curve. I had become a Christian back in 1980, shortly after recovering from an accidental drug overdose—and near-death experience—a resurrection only the power of God could have accomplished. I knew I'd been given a second chance. Years later, still emerging from the vestiges of my old gay identity and the shame and self-hatred associated with it, the diagnosis of HIV+ put me right back into the shadow of imminent death. The sudden prognosis presented me with a new host of destructive thoughts...and feelings: despair, fear, intense anxiety and abandonment.

Gratefully, the persistent prayers from dear brothers and sisters helped quell the bombardment of those depressing thoughts. Substantive hope and peace began to be restored. More and more, I learned to confront those deadly attacks by exercising my authority in Christ.

Just before I tested positive, I had begun volunteering with Desert Stream Ministries. At the same time, I continued to pursue an acting/modeling/waiting-on-tables career. Eventually, I came on fulltime as head of Desert Stream's AIDS outreach, originally called A.R.M., and later renamed Embracing Life.

It seemed like I sort of stumbled into AIDS ministry. I had no special training, medical or ministerial. I just knew there was hope for people with AIDS and God loved them. Hey! My testimony was proof of that. I was more aware of the psychological motives I had for pursuing acting. I had been in it for years—a long time to reflect on why I was driven to do what I did. The motives were not profound or unique: the need for affirmation and acceptance, escape into fantasy, the applause, stardom...everything you've heard from actors before.

MY COMPANION, NOT MY FRIEND

Christian ministry was different and so were the issues (psychological and spiritual) that came up while doing AIDS work. What would eventually become most crucial—the presence of the spirit of death—didn't surface until several years after the ministry started. That discovery began unfolding at a prayer meeting one night when Andrew Comiskey, the director of Desert Stream, suggested with some concern that I appeared unfazed by a string of recent deaths of several AIDS patients. I reacted defensively and was just a little bit insulted. Inside I was thinking, *Hey! Who are you to be questioning how I'm reacting? I don't see you doing this work!* I replied with something like, "I'm just used to death, that's all. Anyway, it's enough to know they're with

It never entered my thoughts...there might be spiritual strategies against my life.

the Lord, in heaven." It was suggested I might be just "a little overly-familiar with death." Awash in self-doubt and confusion, I left. All the way home I questioned the Lord and myself: *Was Andrew right? I thought I had a gift for tolerating death around me? Were things surfacing from my childhood, family, generational stuff? God, am I cold-hearted? What's going on here?*

The ensuing months proved pivotal in my life and for the ministry. The Lord kept bringing to mind one memory after another revealing a major pattern in my life—of making false peace with death. The most difficult times came, however, when pride would try to prevent me from honestly naming it. Finally, I had to name and confront it for what it was—DEATH—and command it to leave. When old thought and feeling patterns would re-emerge, I'd complain, "Surely I don't have to do this again!" Then, with each confrontation, if I stopped to listen, the Lord's words would come to mind: *I have come that they may have life, and have it to the full* (John 10:10). One thing I knew for sure—I hadn't yet tasted enough life to satisfy me. I wanted more! Freedom and determination came from the hunger for more: "Taste and see that the Lord is good..." (Ps. 34:8).

PEELING THE ONION

There were many layers of falsehood about life and God to get through. Evil was never named in my family. As I thought back on my childhood, it never entered my thoughts—or likely my parents'— that there might be spiritual strategies against my life. To my knowledge, my parents didn't have an in-depth relationship with Christ, so Jesus' help was never requested when trouble occurred. The subject of death was never discussed. In my senior year of high school my mother and two friends died. There was no one who was available or who offered to help me sort through the painful loss and confusion. I had to deal with it on my own. A succession of deaths, followed. My own near-death experience from the drug overdose left an indelible impression on my soul. My family's multi-generational denial and avoidance of the subject of death assured I'd be unlikely to confront it. Given the numerous ways my mind and heart had been influenced by death, the Lord graciously revealed the truth at a pace I could deal with. Little by little, He gave me understanding of how the enemy's schemes and deceit had kept me in the dark when it came to experiencing true Life.

Session One:
Jonathan Hunter: My Personal Odyssey of Discovery

Questions for Discussion & Reflection

(Group leaders before reading Jonathan's testimony or sharing your own, ask the participants to listen carefully for experiences in their own lives that may be similar.)

- From what has been shared this far, what similar circumstances can you recall in your history that negatively affected your perceptions of life?

- In what way did the testimony throw new light on the extent to which the spirit of death may be affecting you?

Prayer
Leader prays out loud

We thank You and bless You for all You are going to do in our lives through Your resurrection power to free us from death's influence. We speak out our thanksgiving now.

The leader encourages the group to individually pray out their thanks. As the participants individually pray, the leader may choose to go around the circle and quietly bless each person—not necessarily in the order of the ones praying—laying a hand on their head and anointing them with oil.

Bring closure to the session by blessing the group and sealing all God has done.

Journal

In your prayers during the week note any destructive influences God brings to mind. Thank Him for the Holy exchange He is bringing: beauty for ashes, life for death, and joy for mourning.

Session Two

Unmasking the spirit of death

———*∞∞*———

**The enemy pursues me, he crushes me to
the ground; he makes me dwell in darkness
like those long dead.** Psalm 143:3

The term "spirit of death," may be foreign to some. I
have come to define it as a spiritual influence, a shadow
over our days that veils the way we view life, subverts our
perceptions and shapes a fatalistic mindset. It is not actual
physical death that results from accident, disease or old
age, although that is part of its design and consequence,
but rather the spiritual essence and atmosphere of a fallen
world emanating from the god of this world. As stated in
1 John 5:19, "the whole world is under the control of the
evil one."

Charles H. Kraft, author, former professor (Fuller
Theological Seminary) and minister in the area of inner-
healing and deliverance, has observed a hierarchy of
sorts with spirits. Just as the Lord has a hierarchy of gov-
ernance—archangels, angels, cherubim, seraphim—the
enemy mimics God's government with his fallen archangels
in charge of lesser powers. The spirit of death commands a
constellation of other spirits, all of them ultimately serving
the evil one, Satan. They conspire to destroy a person's life

and attempt to separate them from God. In that state, the enemy's desire is that we will conclude that God is *NOT*: He is *not* sufficient, *not* able, and *not* caring. The enemies of our soul hope that we will turn from seeking the Creator and instead seek the created—people, substances, objects, fantasies—to get our needs met. The net effect is that we feel unreachable, ill-equipped, and unlovable.

The distortion of our beliefs about God originate when we are infants or as young children in reaction to our parents' neglect, rejection, abuse, absence, or simply lack of parenting skills. Our rebellious choices are based on faulty assumptions that our heavenly father is just like our parents. It keeps us perpetually in the dark about life's true possibilities.

A DEADLY STRATEGY

As Christians, we know there are two kingdoms (Matt. 12:25-28): one of light, one of darkness; one of life and one of death. In Colossians 1:13, we read that the Father has "qualified us to share in the inheritance of the saints in the kingdom of light. For he has rescued us from the dominion of darkness and brought us into the kingdom of the Son he loves" (Col. 1:12,13). Or said

The enemies of our soul hope that we will turn from seeking the creator...

another way, "he has delivered us from the power of darkness, and has translated us into the kingdom of his dear Son" (AKJV): that translation is both immediate and a process of ongoing revelation. The spirit of death seeks to keep us ignorant and distracts us from exercising the rights and promises that have come with that transaction, igniting an inner dialogue involving the old or false self and/or the enemy.

Destructive voices try to eliminate, refute or ignore Christ's promises of ever-increasing life. Indeed, preceding the Lord's promise of abundant life in John 10:10, He states, "The thief [Satan] comes only to steal and kill and destroy." Our enemy's minions and systemic propaganda accentuate thoughts of death and destruction, i.e., helplessness, hopelessness, and worthlessness. Death's "bad news" opposes the liberating gospel of the Cross and the fullness of life that Jesus Christ provides. However, unlike the Lord, the devil is not omnipresent. Whenever we sense this deadly presence, we can assume in most cases that we are not being harassed by Satan, himself. Rather, we are encountering an atmosphere of death, influenced by demonic strongholds and supported by cultural and personal belief systems.

The term "spirit of death" best describes (for our purposes) the influential effects of all of death's manifestations—the feeling of separation from God. Some familiar and similar terms can be found in Scripture: "darkness," "the power of the grave," "days of darkness," "sentence of death," and "spirit of despair." Isaiah 25:7 speaks of, "the shroud that enfolds all peoples, the sheet that covers all nations." Isaiah 9:2 alludes to "the shadow of death," as does Psalm 23.

Session Two:
Unmasking the spirit of death

Questions for Discussion & Reflection

- What about the description of the two kingdoms and their spiritual hierarchies was new for you? How does it apply to your personal experience with God?

- If you experienced a disconnect from your parents or God as a child, what do you think happened that led to that sense of separation?

Prayer

Leader instructs the group to break into pairs. Have each person, in turn, confess their fears to God regarding being set free from the spirit of death and its influences, ending with thanksgiving and praise to God for the deliverance He will bring. Prayer partner simply listens and responds by blessing the healing God will accomplish.

Leader concludes by praying over and blessing the group.

Journal

Read Land of Shadow: Psalm 23 *in* Appendix 1
Reflect, meditate and journal your thoughts, prayers and thanks for the good Shepherd of your soul. Ask God to show you something to thank Him for each day.

Session Three

Christians under the Influence

—⟪∿∿⟫—

Since the children have flesh and blood, he too shared in their humanity so that by his death he might destroy him who holds the power of death—that is, the devil—and free those who all their lives were held in slavery by their fear of death. Heb. 2:14, 15

If we belong to God, how can our lives be influenced, held back, strangled, cut off by this spirit of death? What about the Scriptures that proclaim "So if the Son sets you free, you will be free indeed" (John 8:36) and "the old has gone, the new has come" (2 Cor. 5:17)? What about Christ coming to "proclaim freedom for the captives" (Isa. 61:1) and so on?

A combination of factors make us vulnerable: not knowing what Christ accomplished on the Cross or the authority we have as believers; passivity; emotional, mental and verbal habits; unconfessed sin; inner vows and unforgiveness, among others. It is as if we had lived in a broken-down hovel. Then we came into a relationship with God through Christ and were given the deed to a mansion with a beautiful garden and all that goes with it. We either never realized what we'd been given or for some reason, when we made the move, we took our old trappings, furniture, and clothing with us (all the old perceptions, feelings, beliefs, twisted and formed by a spirit of death). Thus we couldn't experience fully what we'd been given. John and Paula Sanford have said "human free will is so precious to our Lord that he will not let the efficacy of the Cross be applied to us without our consent."

This reminds me of a cartoon I find particularly apt that shows a dog chained to its tiny doghouse. In the background, one can make out the large house of the owner. A mesmerized cat sits next to the dog hanging on to its every word. The caption has the dog saying: "They don't keep YOU on a leash because they WANT you to run away." It is an amusing picture of our predicament. The dog (Satan for our purposes) is on a leash. The cat (representative of many a Christian) is clearly free to roam at will, to go in and out of the house (our heavenly Father's), yet is deceived by the cunning and lies of an envious enemy. Not exercising its privileges (and authority) to walk away free, the cat (us) remains in proximity of peril.

WHY IT GETS TO US

> ***...He was a murderer from the beginning,
> not holding to the truth, for there is no truth
> in him. When he lies, he speaks his native
> language, for he is a liar and the father of
> lies."*** John 8:44b

This deadly deceit can affect us in profound and personal ways by keying into our diseased thought patterns and habits. The enemy, the deceiver is familiar with human fallenness in all its forms. He should be; he was there at its inception in the Garden of Eden! Our enemy and his servants use that inside information to taunt us, lie to us and slander us at any given moment. He is the deceiver.

Unfortunately, we are only too ready to agree with him. Unless our false ways of thinking and resulting actions are named, repented of and consistently renounced, our relationship with the Lord and our quality of life will continue to suffer. We must confront unhealed, distorted and erroneous thoughts about God and our identification with depression, anxiety, rejection, self-hatred, loneliness, hopelessness, despair, death fantasies.... These all consume a tremendous amount of time, energy and imagination. They are collectively a "house made of thoughts," as author

[O]ur Lord...will not let the efficacy of the Cross be applied to us without our consent.

Francis Frangipane describes them—creative space the Lord would rather occupy with His TRUTH and LIFE. The dismantling of old thought structures cannot be a passive exercise; we have to participate with the Lord in their undoing.

Session Three:
Christians under the Influence

Questions for Discussion & Reflection

- What are the defective building blocks of your "house made of thoughts"? (For example, not knowing your authority in Christ, mental/emotional/verbal habits, rejection, self-hatred, passivity, etc.)

- How has your life suffered because of wrong thinking/believing based on the spirit of death's misinformation?

Prayer
Leader prays over group

Father, we come before You admitting that we have many habitual, negative and destructive thoughts that we spend a lot of time dwelling on. We acknowledge that they do not produce life. We declare them barren and ungodly. We ask You to help us identify and name them now, giving You permission to begin the process of removing them.

> *Leader directs participants to name out loud the thoughts that are surfacing.*

> *In closing, leader prays out loud in easy to repeat (1-6 word) phrases, asking participants to follow.*

Lord, I want to make room for what is true, noble, right, pure, lovely, admirable, excellent, or praiseworthy—room for Your thoughts and imagination. I acknowledge that with the Cross of Christ I can have victory over the enemy

and the harassment of ungodly thoughts. I declare my mind and emotions subject to the Lordship of Jesus Christ. I declare, Father, You <u>will</u> finish the work You've begun in me. I commit myself to the process of transformation You are accomplishing in me, Lord. I give You thanks for what You are doing in me even now! "Christ in me, the hope of glory." Amen

> *Bless the group and seal all that God has done.*

Journal

> *Each day, write down two things to thank God for (needs met, beauty in nature, relationships, moments of peace, clarity, new understanding, comfort).*

Session Four

When It Begins

—⁓—

The tongue has the power of life and death.
Proverbs 18:21

The origins of our perceptions and imaginings (good or bad) go back to our childhood for the most part—memories forgotten or repressed, including how, when, where and from whom we got them. The immense impact of words and pronouncements (blessing and cursing) from adults who raised us and taught us, compounded by remarks and bullying from our peers, cannot be overstated. Our sponge-like souls absorbed everything we heard; we believed what was said about us was true.

[W]e experience reality distorted by unredeemed thinking...

Life was straightforward and literal to our undiscerning minds. Hurtful names, so lightly tossed out in spite by others, seared our personhood. Harmful words created havoc with our internal perceptions of self: idiot, klutz, bastard, whore, slut, good-for-nothing... the list goes on and on. In the *Three Battlegrounds*, Frances Frangipane observes:

Their thoughtless words went so deep that, in recoiling from the pain, you have involuntarily remained in the recoiled or withdrawn position. Since then, you have refused to place yourself where you can become vulnerable to criticism. You may not even remember the incidents, but you may not have stopped recoiling, even until today.

DAMAGED "GOODNESS"

Poisonous words wound the soul and accumulate in the mind occupying ever-increasing space. Over time, they become an interior fortress of sorts; the price paid for its maintenance is a severe tax on one's well being. This formidable collection casts a shadow of bitterness and disappointment over gifts and sacraments the Lord intended to convey life. Words that God intended to impart comfort and assurance—to reflect his steadfast commitment and love—begin to carry a negative connotation after passing through our experiential grid:

Birth   "I (they) wish I had never been born."
Family   "It was never safe. We always fought."
Marriage "Entrapment."
Home   "It was a house I couldn't wait to leave."
Intimacy "If they really got to know me, they'd reject me."

In my life, there were many areas that were fuel for disappointment: a confused sexual identity, unhappily married parents, alcoholic father, drugs, death of friends and mother, HIV infection, and a multigenerational pattern of illness, suicide and unacknowledged sin—strongholds for the spirit of death.

Depression, chronic illness, self-hatred, introspection, hopelessness, and self destruction associated with the spirit of death can result from a variety of experiences: birth traumas (being the child of rape, an unwanted pregnancy or failed abortion); suicide attempts; crippling or isolating childhood diseases; violent or emotionally abusive homes; caring for chronically ill family members; death of cherished loved ones; witnessing or having deadly tragedies happen to you, your immediate/extended family or ethnic group; rejection because of faith and gender; and countless other life-altering events or situations. Many who would appear to have had very happy childhoods and lives, may also have been just as affected. It's how we experience reality distorted by unredeemed thinking that causes us to fall prey to living in the valley of the shadow of death.

Session Four:
When it Begins

Questions for Discussion & Reflection

- In what manner did your family environment shape your perceptions of birth, family, marriage, home and intimacy?

- What lingering family myths, pronouncements by others over you, curses, inner vows (e.g., I'll never be angry like my father/mother) have influenced the way you live?

Prayer

Leader explains to group that in the following prayer they will be asking God to remind them of the curses, vows or pronouncements that have been spoken over them and those they have directed toward themselves and others.

Leader prays in short phrases (as before) with participants repeating...

Lord, I ask You to continue to reveal the damaging and destructive influences that have marred my perception of Your sacraments and institutions. As You reveal past myths from my family, inner vows I've made, curses and pronouncements made over me, I invite You to help me in renouncing them and refusing them a place in my life again!

Invite participants to renounce those vows, pronouncements, curses, etc., out loud in the group.

*In closing, leader prays out loud (as before)
with participants repeating...*

Lord, I need to fill my mind and heart with Your words of encouragement. I invite You now to be Lord over my thoughts and affections. Open my spiritual ears to hear Your voice, now, and in the future, replacing that which is false with that which is true. In the name of Jesus Christ I pray. Amen

Journal

Each day in prayer, ask the Father:

Redeem my past. Help me to see family, home, intimacy, marriage, (my) birth, through Your eyes. Resurrect my vision for life. Replace the pronouncements and curses spoken over me with Your words of truth. I wait on You...

*Write down in your journal any thoughts that
may surface.*

Session Five

Operating Under the Influence

—◦◦◦—

The purposes of a person's heart are deep waters, but one who has insight draws them out. Proverbs 20:5

M any of us grow up viewing God's creation through a cloud of unbelief—cataracts that prevent us from perceiving and experiencing life more fully. Our over-identification with dark thoughts and faulty assumptions about God reinforce a jaded worldview, resulting in impoverished relationships (beginning with God) and ineffective ministries. It is no wonder the world is unimpressed by so much of what we're about as Christians; we go about life with such low expectations.

It is a sad irony that some serving in the helping professions are totally unaware that they are operating under death's influence... precisely because they are under it! They've chosen careers at hospitals, convalescent centers, in hospice care, or social services because of a familiarity with sickness, ability to tolerate death, or because they are drawn to help those needier than themselves. [Refer to Jonathan's story in Session One.] It needs to be said that those working outside of healing professions may have made their choices out of hopelessness, helplessness, or worthlessness informed by the spirit of death. For example, it may have been required they continue in the family business or pursue the vocational choice expected of them.

What motivated *your* job choice: financial security, social acceptability, family expectations, or peer pressure? Consider too, the basis for your relationships: are they open and healthy? Are you part of a Christian community where you can hear and speak the truth in love? Are you equally comfortable sharing or receiving in your friendships? We need to look at our motives and impetus. Are our choices made out of an abundance of life in Christ, or because of our identification with things associated with death? Proverbs 16:2 says: "All a man's motives seem innocent to him, but motives are weighed by the Lord." So often our primary vocational and personal relationships are tied in with our desire to make right what went wrong in our childhood. If we are willing to go before the Lord for an examination of our inner motivations, we might be surprised at what He uncovers.

> *Unbelief—cataracts that prevent us from perceiving and experiencing life more fully.*

Session Five:
Operating Under the Influence

Questions for Discussion & Reflection

- What career or line of work have you chosen or do you aspire to?

- What influenced your choice(s)? Were you pressured into a career, or did your decisions and actions issue out of a God-given passion or skill?

- Discuss any vocational or relational choices connected to "righting what went wrong" in your family?

Prayer

Leader instructs the participants to break out into pairs. Each person takes 10 minutes to share with their partner the negative career and relational drivers that may have surfaced for them during the teaching and sharing times. Further direct them that when each person finishes, their partner is to simply bless them, proclaiming God's good future and hope over them (Jer. 29:11).

After all the pairs are finished, have them rejoin the larger group.

In closing, leader prays out loud (as before) with participants repeating...

Lord, I have presented myself and my choices to You. I have asked and will continue to ask You to weigh them. I choose to trust in You, Lord, that You will guide me in the

way everlasting as I relinquish my plans to You. I thank You for the Body of Christ of which I am a member; I thank You that it is my rich source of nurture and counsel. Finally, Lord, I thank You that I have a destiny in fulfilling Your will on earth, and You will see it through to completion, as I give all my ways over to You. Amen

Journal

> *Ask God to reveal the passions and aspirations you may have buried. Then write them down and offer them to the Father in prayer, thanking Him for redeeming all that was lost.*

Session Six

Breaking Free

—⁓—

If you hold to my teaching, you are really my disciples. Then you will know the truth, and the truth will set you free. John 8:31b, 32

Familiar fearful thoughts have convinced a lot of us that to take up arms against our foe will only lead to disappointment and failure, maybe even harm. Convinced of this lie, many of us have become spiritually apprehensive and sedentary when it comes to exercising our authority in Christ. Because we Christians have the potential of doing the most damage to the enemy, immobilized is exactly how the devil wants to keep us!

Getting free is not a simple one-time act or prayer, though the answer and means for achieving it can be simply put—Jesus Christ. The liberation we seek is and will be a process, an ongoing and progressive one achieved with the Lord. Getting free is all about Christ's authority in us. It says in Proverbs 9:10: "The fear of the Lord is the beginning of wisdom and knowledge of the Holy One is understanding" [emphasis mine]. Implied here is the necessity for an intimate, abiding experience (union) with the Holy Spirit. Indeed, we must habitually nurture our relationship with the Lord of life before we can effectively recognize and overcome the spirit of death. As C. S. Lewis writes in his book *Miracles*, this is possible because of what the Lord has already done:

> *He is the "first fruits," the "pioneer of life." He has forced open a door that has been locked since the death of the first man. He has met, fought, and beaten the King of Death. Everything is different because He has done so.*

BY HIS STRENGTH AND AUTHORITY

> ***Jesus said, "I am the way, the truth and the life*."** John 14:6

> ***"I am the Living One; I was dead and behold I am alive for ever and ever! I hold the keys of death and Hades*."** Rev. 1:18

It is all about the authority and strength of Christ to deliver us from destructive ways, just as St. Paul writes: "I can do all things through Christ who strengthens me" (Phil. 4:13 NKJV).

Dr. Charles Kraft has written extensively on the authority of Christ, emphasizing the necessity for Christians to understand and utilize that authority to live free from demonic harassment. In his books and seminars he often recounts the story of a woman who had been deeply involved in the occult and later became a Christian. She was able to share some valuable insights into occult activity and abilities. Most occultists, she said, understood and exercised the power they knew they possessed. Furthermore, they could "see" in the spirit realm those who didn't—namely Christians. They took special pleasure in intimidating unsuspecting

Christians on the street with a look or a shove. However, she noted, every so often they would spot trouble coming—someone clearly aware of their authority in Christ. She, and those like her, took pains to avoid anyone who walked in that authority, even crossing to the other side of the street to get out of their way.

PUTTING ON CHRIST

Since the birth, death and resurrection of Jesus Christ, the conflict with death has taken on new dimensions. A regenerated humanity has appeared on the field—God's enlistment to bring about His ultimate victory. No longer able to helplessly claim, "I'm only human," humanity has been given Godly strength in union with Christ. Through the Holy Spirit, God's mighty power is at work within to rebuff, attack, and expel ungodliness. The apostle Paul models this new identity (as God's warrior) in his letter to the church at Corinth: "We

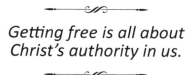

Getting free is all about Christ's authority in us.

demolish arguments and every pretension that sets itself up against the knowledge of God, and we take captive every thought to make it obedient to Christ" (2 Cor. 10:5). Paul's use of the present tense tells us that the encroachment of ungodly thoughts and ideas is an act of attempted control we humans *must continually battle* albeit in Christ. Again, to the Corinthians: "For He must reign [through us] until He has put all His enemies under His feet. The last enemy to be destroyed is death" (1 Cor. 15:26).

It is important to note that elsewhere, as in James 1:14,15, we read how our willful choices, consciously or not, can prolong the conflict: "But each one is tempted when he is drawn away by his own desires and enticed. Then, when desire has conceived it gives birth to sin; and sin, when it is full-grown, *brings forth* death" [emphasis mine]. Indeed, there is an enemy on the prowl looking for the right moment to move in. Thus our fallen ways of thinking, believing and acting bring forth our enemy, giving him the right to harass us! We cannot afford to be passively resistant in the face of such attacks. We must "Resist him, standing firm in the faith" (1 Pet. 5:8,9).

No matter who we are, we all come up against the presence of death in some form or another. Paul alludes to feeling "the sentence of death" in his heart. What we see repeated over and over in these Scriptures is God revealing our weakness in the face of sin and death, and our need to be fully dependent on Him for redemption and deliverance.

Session Six:
Breaking Free...

Questions for Discussion & Reflection

- How has evil's depiction (and its power) in the media influenced the way you perceive and respond to it?

- What have you been taught about your authority in Christ and how to exercise it in your everyday life?

Prayer

> *Leader directs group to* Appendix II: "The Authority of Christ."*

> *Have the participants look over the list of Scriptures. Encourage them to speak out in random order the ones that inspire them. (Repetition is fine. There will be lots of it.)*

> *In closing, leader prays out loud in short phrases (as before) with participants repeating...*

Father of Glory, give me the Spirit of wisdom and revelation in the knowledge of Christ. Let the eyes of my understanding be enlightened, that I may know what is the hope of Your calling and what are the riches of the glory of Christ's inheritance in me, and what is the exceeding greatness of Your power toward me and those who believe, according to the working of Your mighty power which You worked in Christ when You raised Him from the dead and seated Him at Your right hand in the heavenly places, far above all principality and power and might and dominion, and every name that is named, not only

in this age, but also in the age which is to come. Amen (*paraphrase of* Eph. 1:17-21).

Journal

> *Review the Scripture List in* Appendix II *and write down any other Scripture verses that you find that speak of the authority we possess in Christ.*

Session Seven

Staying Free

—⁓—

He has delivered us from such a deadly peril and he will deliver us. On him we have set our hope that he will continue to deliver us, as you help us by your prayers. 2 Cor. 1:10,11

"For I know the plans I have for you," declares the sovereign Lord, "plans to prosper you and not to harm you, plans to give you hope and a future." Jer. 29:11

I've seen countless individuals set free from the contaminating torment that held them for so long. Once out from under that oppressive yoke, they begin their awakened life by making death their enemy (as it is to Christ). They continue to do so by repeatedly renouncing the spirit of death whenever they sense its familiar influence encroaching upon their lives. That is how one attains and sustains freedom from its effects, along with the obvious need for resting in God's strength, love and authority. Being creatures of habit, however, we all too quickly fall back into familiar, destructive ways of framing our perceptions and opinions about circumstances and people. It takes persistence in prayer and a resolute God-empowered will to live free from those old influences. The following is a brief testimony from one who has learned the process of getting free:

I had renounced the spirit of death numerous times, particularly as it related to my struggle with self-hatred and various fears. Recently, the Lord brought back to mind a season when I was bulimic. In the prayer time, I saw that I partnered with the spirit of death in my self-destruction. I had never truly repented of this. As I grieved over my sin, one particular memory was incredibly clear. In it I saw the cross very near me. The Lord invited me to turn to the cross—to Him—rather than to my self-destructive coping mechanisms. I had the choice between life and death. Though I had chosen death, He was offering me the opportunity to repent and choose life. I then asked the Lord what could be done about the inner pain that was driving my bulimia. Kneeling beside me, He said I wasn't meant to bear the pain. But He was. I could lean into Him and He could bear it. Immediately I felt great joy and comfort. I saw the death that came from bearing the pain apart from Christ. I found comfort and release as I leaned into Him with my grief, entering into His care and receiving His life in exchange. C.M.

> *Praying together is part of the rhythm of living free...*

Make no mistake about it; the Lord is faithful. He will reveal the extent of the enemy's schemes and help us to overcome him if we ask: "Death is naked before God; destruction lies uncovered" (Job 26:6).

REACHING OUT TO OTHERS

Is anyone among you in trouble? He should pray. Is anyone happy? Let him sing songs of praise. Is any one of you sick [without strength, weak, feeble or diseased]? He should call for the elders of the church to pray over him and anoint him with oil in the name of the Lord. And the prayer offered in faith will make the sick person well and the Lord will raise him up. If he has sinned, he will be forgiven. Therefore confess your sins to each other and pray for each other so that you may be healed [made whole]. The prayer of a righteous man is powerful and effective. James 5:13-15

Once I [Jonathan] made the decision not to support the destructive influences of the spirit of death, I started getting a little distance from its accompanying thoughts through repeated renunciation. The prayers with brothers and sisters who readily pointed out my "stinkin' thinkin'" became indispensable. Of course, one has to give permission to others to speak into one's life when ungodliness raises its ugly head. But once we do, assertively praying together will send those thoughts and spirits to flight.

Praying together is part of the rhythm of living free from the influence of the spirit of death. The enemy's tactic for wearing us down and eliminating us is to separate us from the support of the body of Christ. Think *National Geographic* and the way the lion stalks the lonely gazelle separated from the herd. You get the idea. It would have been impossible without my church family's advocacy to overcome that invisible, chronic influence; the power of their prayers has been my lifeline.

WHY PRAYER WITH OTHERS IS IMPORTANT

At Embracing Life conferences, trainings, workshops, and in private sessions, we always speak the prayer of renunciation out loud. Why? Our declaration is made together before a "cloud of witnesses." It is a reminder to the enemy that we are not alone in our proclamation. Later on, the enemy (and the old or "false self") may come back with the same old lies and accusations: *You're not going to pray that again, are you? You did it once, already! You should be beyond that by now!* But this simply presents another opportunity for us to declare the truth that we have been set free in Christ.

Creation will truly live completely free from those destructive influences the day death is thrown into the lake of fire (Rev. 20:14). Until then, we will have to be vigilant and consistent in renouncing the spirit of death until it no longer finds us a welcoming place to hang around. We need courage and persistence to engage our will to that end... but we *must* engage, again and again. Proverbs 15:24 says, "The pathway of life leads upward for the wise to keep him from going down to the grave." We need to build up our spiritual muscle for the climb. Our God will supply all of our strength for the journey in order to fulfill the work He has begun (Phil. 1:6)!

Session Seven:
Staying Free

Questions for Discussion & Reflection

- What are your concerns about letting others know your needs and asking them to pray for you in overcoming the spirit of death? (Example: I would appear weak, negative, or hyper-spiritual....)

- Renowned Christian author Henry Nouwen has written that we are all "wounded healers." Share a time when you have prayed for someone else in the midst of your own brokenness and need for healing. Why do you think this is an important part of your faith walk?

Prayer

Leaders have the participants break into pairs. Each person will have an opportunity to ask God to empower them to actively engage in renouncing the spirit of death, consistently, whenever it intrudes in his or her own life or the life of others. The listening partner will then bless the commitment to prayer..

In closing, leader prays out loud in short phrases (as before) with participants repeating...

Lord, we declare that we are staying in the battle and not giving up. We come as a body united in this pledge of allegiance to You, proclaiming with confidence Your ability to deliver us. We acknowledge You as our strength and means to get free and stay free from the influence of

the enemy of our soul. Once again, we declare You, Jesus Christ, as the Lord of Life—triumphant over all the powers. Your work on the Cross will forever remain the defining act that has enabled humankind to share in Your resurrection power and to overcome the spirit of death and all its influences. To You, forever be the praise and glory of our salvation, *and* our freedom. Amen

Bless the group and seal all that God has done.

Journal

Consider any new understanding or healing the Lord has given you through the More Life! *sessions thus far. Write a letter of thanksgiving and appreciation to Him. In faith, end by affirming your expectation for more and greater healing.*

Session Eight

Evicting the Squatters

—~⁓~—

"Now is the time for judgment on this world; now the prince of this world will be driven out." John 12:31

"Who will rescue me from this body of death? Thanks be to God— through Jesus Christ our Lord!" writes Apostle Paul (Rom. 7:24,25). I can state confidently that it is possible to live free from the persistent presence of the spirit of death—in *all* its forms—through the authority of Jesus Christ. You and I will proclaim along with Paul, "Where O death is your sting? Where, O death is your victory?" (1 Cor. 15:55)

Our Father in heaven desires that His children enjoy the increasing fullness of His Presence (Heb. 2:14,15). Every day He calls us to appropriate, by faith, the abundant life so richly poured out by His Son through the Holy Spirit. When we pray the prayer of renunciation, we are in essence inviting the Lord to clean out the moneychangers within us, His temple (see Matt. 21:12,13). As He goes at it, the Holy Spirit reveals to us the "squatters," if you will, of unrighteousness that are feeding off our unconscious mind. The piercing light and knowledge that can only come from the Lord Himself exposes these parasites. As they are revealed to us, the Lord merely asks us to participate in evicting them. There can be no excuses, no bargaining or concessions. Make no false peace with darkness.

OUT OF TOUCH WITH YOUR STUFF

This is where pride of thought and image can come to play. Some of us just aren't ready to have that deception exposed. It hurts our pride to think that, as Christians, we could have harbored such thoughts and motives for so long. For others, the idea of darkness and light existing side by side within doesn't fit into their theology (refer to 1 John 1:8-10). Here's a good example of what I'm talking about:

Over the years my work as a nurse often involved prayer for the dying. I was at peace with the idea that people on this side of eternity don't live forever, and while mildly curious, I saw no need to pursue the 'spirit of death' thing.... I suppose it was my pride and my stubbornness that resisted the truth—I was in fact living under the influence of the spirit of death. When you [Jonathan] began to lead in renouncing the spirit of death, my initial response was, I don't need this. ...Then I reconsidered, thinking, I guess I can pray along with this guy. After all, what could it hurt?

The result was amazing. I had no idea how distorted my thinking had become until a few days after following your lead in renouncing [death]. I realized I no longer obsessed over who would sing what songs and what Scriptures would be read at my memorial service. I stopped wondering if I needed to change my will. I quit internally debating whether to have my ashes buried or scattered. D.K.

GOOD INTENTIONS / GRIM RESULTS

There may be some of you who have made treaties with illness itself (though you thought it was with God). You asked that a loved one be freed from their illness so that you might carry it instead. This is what is called a substitutionary vow. Though sincerely made, this is sincerely mistaken. Christ is our

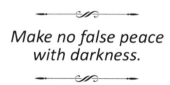

Make no false peace with darkness.

substitute. He bears our wounds; it is by His stripes that we are healed (Isa. 53:4-6). Be warned. If we ask to be made ill in another's place, the enemy is only too happy to oblige the invitation. The result may be two sick people instead of one. We can carry another's burden in prayer, but we must not take on their illness with it.

WHAT GOD CAN REVEAL...

I mentioned earlier in my testimony that generational patterns of destructive thought and action were revealed to me in the healing process. For some of you, similar histories may be exposed in prayer such as premature deaths over generations, recurring illnesses (cancer, heart disease, diabetes...), familial curses, criminal activity, occultism and the like. Cautionary advice here: don't go digging for it. God will surface what you need to know about destructive aspects of your family history. When He does, simply thank Him for revealing it, affirm the power of the Cross over death and receive His transforming life in return.

A final point before we pray: This booklet is intended to be a tool. It is a basic one to assist you in better understanding what may have been plaguing you for some time. Even if you are still unclear as to whether the spirit of death is a serious problem for you, *please pray The Prayer!* It is not a mantra. It simply reflects spiritual principles and scriptural truth. Its power is not in the exact words, but the Living Word, Jesus. Edit what you will; it can serve as a framework from which to model a prayer of your own. Use it to pray with others who are struggling with this issue. Pray it OUT LOUD with them. You'll be the better for it.

The Prayer

Leader prays in short phrases (as before) with participants repeating...

✧ **I am not born of "natural descent, nor of human decision or a husband's will, but born of God"** (John 1:13).

✧ **I am born of "imperishable seed"** (1 Pet. 1:23).

✧ **"I can do all things through Christ who strengthens me"** (Phil. 4:13 NKJV).

✧ **Heavenly Father, Lord Jesus Christ and Holy Spirit, I come before You with my fellow brothers and sisters as witnesses to declare my freedom from the spirit of death and its influences.**

✧ **By the power and authority granted me by my Lord Jesus Christ, and in whose name I pray, I renounce the spirit of death and all unclean spirits associated with it. I declare any and all attachments, agreements, appeasements and treaties with those spirits nullified and cancelled. Henceforth I will make no false peace with my enemy.**

✞ I renounce all identification, activity and preoccupation with the following: suicidal thoughts, death fantasies, illness, despair, worthlessness, hopelessness, helplessness, perfectionism, fatalism, depression, isolationism, legalism, abandonment, passivity, bitterness, rage, anxiety, fear, poverty, rejection, violence, racism, and medical pronouncements of impending death. Separate them from me, now, Lord, as far as the East is from the West.

✞ I sever with the sword of the Spirit of Truth, any attachments to generational spirits going back ten generations, placing the Cross of Jesus Christ between me and each one of them.

✞ I repent of any substitutionary vows, reasserting that it is by Jesus Christ's sacrifice and sufferings that I and my loved ones are saved and healed.

✞ I will make a conscious effort to forgive all those who knowingly or unknowingly wounded me and thereby enabled death to gain influence over me. I ask You Lord to give me ongoing revelation as to whom I need to forgive.

✞ Forgive me Lord for holding onto unforgiveness, anger, hatred, judgment, pride, bitterness, revenge and any other sinful reaction against those people and, most importantly, You. I will continue to release them and the feelings as You make them known to me. And I release You Lord from judgments that You are in any way insufficient, ineffectual, or indifferent with regard to me and my needs. Forgive me for being blind to Your true character and loving nature.

✞ I receive from You, Lord, the cleansing of Your forgiveness.

✝ Please continue to reveal any other hidden, destructive influences in and over my life, so that I may send them to Your Cross to be nailed there.

✝ I will, by Your strength, Your love, Your power, and in Your authority, continue to confess, repent, renounce and resist the spirit of death and its associates, by aligning my will with Yours. I proclaim Your will for me is to know abundant life.

✝ Now I choose to embrace the fullness of life You have for me, Lord.

✝ I praise You and thank You for always upholding and covering me in Your everlasting love. Amen

In the moments that follow, allow time for the Holy Spirit to surface those people, thoughts, influences, and experiences that need to be released to the Cross. Wind down the ministry time by praying out loud:

✝ Jesus, come and make Your authoritative Presence known to me. Now, where death has been, reveal Your life in me.

Pause to allow the Lord to reveal Himself to those gathered. Leader may want to repeat the invitation. Give ample time for the Lord to uniquely touch each person.

The leader and participants ask the Holy Spirit to seal the work He has done:

✝ Holy Spirit, I ask You to seal out all that I have repented of and seal in the abundant life You have given me in exchange. Amen.

In groups, members may wish to repeat the following Scriptures with the leader adding any other appropriate prayer directives in Jesus' name—especially the need to repeat The Prayer *whenever necessary.*

✞ **"I have set before you life and death, blessings and curses. Now choose life, so that you and your children may live and that you may love the Lord your God, listen to his voice, and hold fast to him. For the Lord is your life, and he will give you many years in the land..."** (Dt. 30:19,20).

✞ **"I am the resurrection and the life. He who believes in me will live even though he dies; and whoever lives and believes in me will never die"** (John 11:25).

**Session Eight:
Evicting the Squatters**

Questions for Discussion & Reflection

- What new understanding/revelation of the spirit of death did you receive after praying *The Prayer* at the end of this session—or during the previous seven sessions?

  Give as much time as necessary for group members to share their responses.

  When finished, direct their attention to Appendix III. Have the group look over the comparison lists and present the following questions:

- What stands out most to you?

- Can you identify areas where you've experienced change(s) in the past 8 weeks?

  Complete the discussion time by having the Group look over the Post Prayer Notes for Staying Free *in* Appendix IV. *The leader may underscore any areas they think are of particular significance for the group members.*

Prayer
   In closing, leader prays out loud (as before) with participants repeating...

Father, I bless what You have done and will do in my life through this knowledge. Surely You have revealed Your

wisdom, authority and love for us in exposing the strategy of the enemy and its effect on our lives. Your resurrection power has, is, and will set me free from those influences if I align my will with Yours. I acknowledge that this is not only for my benefit but also for others I meet who may be under the influence. I have pledged to help them engage with the same truth that I have come to know: that You have revealed Yourself in the person of the Lord Jesus Christ that I might have life and have it abundantly. Amen

Bless the group members and all that God has done.

Appendix I

Land of Shadow: Psalm 23

———∾∾∾———

The Lord is my shepherd; I shall not be in want. He makes me lie down in green pastures. He leads me beside quiet waters. He restores my soul. He guides me in the paths of righteousness for His name's sake. Even though I walk through the valley of the shadow of death I will fear no evil, for You are with me. Your rod and Your staff, they comfort me. You prepare a table before me in the presence of my enemies. You anoint my head with oil; my cup overflows. Surely goodness and love will follow me all the days of my life, and I will dwell in the house of the Lord forever. Psalm 23

Psalm 23 is a personal favorite of mine [Jonathan] because of its powerful imagery and compressed drama. In effect, the reader is taken on a telescopic lifetime journey with the Lord. The psalmist's words speak right to the heart, particularly the "valley of the shadow of death" part. Placed in the middle of the psalm, hope and fulfillment hinge on the shepherd's ability to get David (and you and me) through that all-too-familiar place of foreboding. Of course, He does, although for many that truth is hard to grab hold of. It is easy to get fixated on the valley because it so evocatively describes that place on the sojourner's road of life where one often feels stranded—four flat tires, no cell phone, no Auto Club card, no help in sight.

Some of us, because of the ongoing difficulties and pain as we grew up, feel like we were raised in that "valley of the shadow"; as one person put it: "Our family creed was, 'We are acquainted with grief.'" It is a legacy from our parents and we're resigned to it being our lot in life. Sure the location is depressing, but it is real estate! Years of living in that threatening emotional and spiritual place drives some to the erroneous conclusion that it is the Lord's will that they remain there, though nothing could be further from scriptural truth.

It is intended we pass "through" the valley; the Lord never purposed us to remain there. Having passed through it, however, doesn't exempt us from future valley excursions. Jesus exhorts us: "In this world you will have trouble. But take heart! I have overcome the world" (John 16:33). Jesus is the true shepherd of the psalm; His rod and staff bring comfort. Viewed as symbols representing His Cross, the rod signifies Christ's authority, protection, guidance and rescue; the staff, in turn, represents the horizontal of the cross, for us the load bearing support of the Lord throughout our journey in life. Comforting as those words are, for some of us the Lord's goodness noted in the verses surrounding "the valley," is obscured by the ominous "shadow of death," despite the presence of "the" Shepherd. Our frustration is compounded by the shame we experience when, as Christians, we can't summon up an overcoming attitude.

This psalm is a good diagnostic tool for unmasking the spirit of death in our lives, revealing to what degree we are living in its shadow, and ultimately leading us to "life."

Reflection & Meditation:

- Have you ever noticed how many people cite this as one of their favorite psalms? There's a reason: people relate to it. What impresses you most about it?

- Meditate on the words of this psalm, one line at a time. Listen for the Shepherd's voice. Jesus said: "My sheep listen to my voice; I know them, and they follow me" (John 10:27).

Appendix II

The Authority of Christ

All Scriptures are NIV unless otherwise noted

1 John 4:4b Greater is He who is in you than He who is in the world.

1 Cor. 15:55 Where, O death, is your victory? Where O death, is your sting?

1 Cor. 15:56,57 (The Message) It was sin that made death so frightening and law-code guilt that gave sin its leverage, its destructive power. But now in a single victorious stroke of life, all three—sin, guilt, death—are gone, the gift of our Master, Jesus Christ. Thank God.

2 Cor. 1:9,10 In our hearts we felt the sentence of death. But this happened that we might not rely on ourselves but on God, who raises the dead. He has delivered us from such a deadly peril, and he will deliver us.

Rom. 7:24,25 (The Message) I've tried everything and nothing helps. I'm at the end of my rope. Is there no one who can do anything for me? Isn't that the real question?

The answer, thank God, is that Jesus Christ can and does. He acted to set things right in this life of contradictions where I want to serve God with all my heart and mind, but am pulled by the influence of sin to do something totally different.

Rom. 16:20 The God of peace will soon crush Satan under your feet.

Col. 2:15 And having disarmed the powers and authorities, he made a public spectacle of them, triumphing over them by the Cross.

1 Pet. 3:22 Jesus Christ...has gone into heaven and is at God's right hand...with angels, authorities and powers in submission to him.

Matt. 28:18 Jesus...said, "All authority in heaven and on earth has been given to me...Go, therefore...I am with you always..."

1 John 5:18b-21 (The Message) The God-begotten are also the God-protected. The Evil One can't lay a hand on them. We know that we are held firm by God; it's only the people of the world who continue in the grip of the Evil One. And we know that the Son of God came so we would recognize and understand the truth of God—what a gift!—and we are living in the Truth itself, in God's Son, Jesus Christ. This Jesus is both True God and Real Life. Dear children, be on guard against all clever facsimiles.

John 10:28,29 I give them eternal life, and they shall never perish; no one can snatch them out of my hand. My Father, who has given them to me, is greater than all; no one can snatch them out of my Father's hand.

John 14:6 I am the way and the truth and the life.

John 15:7 If you remain in me and my words remain in you, ask whatever you wish, and it will be given you.

Rev. 1:18 I am the Living One: I was dead, and behold I am alive for ever and ever! And I hold the keys of death and Hades.

John 8:31,32 Jesus said, "If you hold to my teaching, you are really my disciples. Then you will know the truth, and the truth will set you free."

1 Cor. 15:25,26 (The Message) Jesus won't let up until the last enemy is down and the very last enemy is death! As the psalmist said, "He laid them low, one and all; He walked all over them."

Appendix III

Fruits of the Holy Spirit vs. Manifestations of the spirit of death

————∞————

This comparative chart is intended as inspiration for prayer, not a guide for introspection. After reviewing it, you can bring issues that emerge to God in prayer.

Holy Spirit	spirit of death
• Truth	• Lies (or the truth distorted)
• Worship	• Introspection
• Freedom, self control	• Compulsion, bondage
• Balanced view	• Distorted view
• Fruitful, expectations often realized	• Unfruitful, expectations cut off
• Able to make plans and follow through	• Difficulty making and completing plans

Continued...

Holy Spirit (cont.)	**spirit of death** (cont.)
• Dreams often fulfilled	• Dreams often unfulfilled or perceived to be unfulfilled.
• Able to cope with frustration and disappointment	• Expects frustration and disappointment
• Embraces life, while aware that death exists.	• Fantasizes about death, dying or suicide, while a vibrant life seems illusive and far off.
• Able to look at health issues objectively and with faith	• Talks about, expects and experiences ill health
• Hope	• Despair, hopelessness
• Compassion	• Narcissism
• Joy	• Depression
• Wholesome sense of humor	• Self-deprecation, cynicism, dark humor
• Mind is clear	• Thoughts and reality seem foggy and gray
• Lives in present, while having objectivity about the past and hope for the future	• Lives in past and future, memory is skewed towards negative events
• Victorious through Christ and the Cross	• Victim of fate, others actions
• Christ conscious, serving others as God directs	• Self absorbed, sometimes codependent

Continued...

Holy Spirit (cont.)	spirit of death (cont.)
• Knows acceptance and worth, valued because of God's love	• Feels rejected and worthless, valued because of what one does or has
• Experiences a range of emotions, from sadness to joy.	• Experiences more negative emotion, sadness, depression, abandonment, helplessness, hopelessness, self-hatred
• Accepts their own failures and those of others, without condemnation	• Perfectionistic and judgmental, finds forgiving themselves and others difficult
• Able to maintain intimate relationships	• Finds intimacy illusive
• Focused on things that are lovely, praiseworthy, of good report	• Obsessed with thoughts, situations, conversations and media that are dark, centered on crime, death, abuse, heartbreak or violence
• Able to deal with life through Christ and community.	• Helpless
• Actively exercising will to rest in Christ	• Passive, damaged will
• Takes responsibility for mistakes, but doesn't get stuck there	• Blames self and others for situations and reruns offenses and disappointments

Your life and actions may be partially or totally whole, healthy and life-centered in one area and shadowed by death in another. Invite the Lord to continue doing a restorative work in you as He wills and you are willing.

Appendix IV

Post-prayer Notes for Staying Free

—ᘐᘐ—

- Embrace life in the person of Jesus Christ. Open yourself to His wonderful love.

- Recognize the influence of the spirit of death in your life and ask God to reveal areas that need prayer.

- Name, confess, and renounce thoughts and feelings that are destructive as often as necessary.

- Cultivate intimate knowledge of your authority in Christ.

- Initiate conversations with God and meditate on His Word. Practice His presence (remembering He is always present and will never leave or forsake you) and listen to His healing words. (See *Bibliography & Suggested Readings* for listening prayer material.)

- Write down and meditate on the truth of who you are as revealed in the Word of God and listening prayer.

- Take opportunity to worship and thank the Lord throughout your day.

- Stay covered by the prayerful support of others.

- Pray for others to get free—then "your healing will quickly appear" (Isa. 58:6-12).

- Stay connected (or get connected) to a church family.

- Learn to rest in the finished work of Christ; lean on His strength.

- Keep short accounts: forgive, repent and reconcile.

   The one who calls you is faithful and he will do it. 1 Thess. 5:24

APPENDIX V

Resources for Group Leaders/Facilitators

—◦∾◦—

We created this book to be used in a group setting or by individuals. We have found that in most cases healing is accelerated and supported in community. So, if possible, we encourage you to share this journey with others. There are many ways to implement this book. Below are just a few.

Scheduling
- Individuals: reading, praying and journaling on a regular annual cycle
- Group: As a 1 day intensive (8-10 hours plus breaks and meals)
- Group: Divided over 2 Saturdays
- Group: Over eight weeks (two-hour sessions)

Group Size
- Any size the facilitator is comfortable with: 2–20, or more
- A very large group could also break into smaller groups for discussion and prayer

Structure

- For weekly meetings, it's helpful to have members read through the sessions before the group meets. The session review discussion questions can be integrated into the reading of the material, or saved until the end.
- The order of elements in the session review can be switched and you can add or reword the questions.
- Leader/Facilitator should bring as many appropriate examples as possible to the session discussion.

Session Review Sample:

Questions for Discussion & Reflection
Usually there are questions relating to the session or thematic discussion points. If you are not in a group setting you can journal these questions and your answers.

Prayer
A different prayer for each session is supplied. Suggestions are given for leaders to begin prayers by reading out loud in short phrases to be repeated by the group participants.

Journal
Scriptures and reflection topics are supplied for journaling.

FURTHER SUGGESTIONS FOR GROUP FACILITATION:

<u>A Critical Reminder</u>: **Group members need to honor confidentiality. What is shared in the group stays in the group!**

If you are facilitating *More Life!*, the following are some suggestions for you to adapt as best fits your gathering.

- Be creative! Adapt the materials to your unique group. Feel free to bring fresh ideas to how you present the material.

- Open with worship and prayer.

- During the week pray for the participants.

- Review the materials for each week ahead of time. Answer the questions yourself.

- Keep to the agreed upon times for each session. Respect the time constraints of those who attend.

- Let God be the counselor. You are a facilitator not a psychologist. If a person needs additional help, refer them to trusted Christian counselors in your area.

- If you have a large group, you may want to break into smaller groups with co-facilitators during the session review.

- ONE OF THE MOST IMPORTANT THINGS YOU CAN CONVEY to each member of your group whether large or small is that God has a different healing journey for each of them. The destination is the same: wholeness, abundant life, joy, peace and an unhindered relationship with God and with others. How God gets us there is tailored to our temperament and history. Encourage them not to compare themselves to another. Consider: The healing work of God is sometimes obvious immediately, but our restoration unfolds over a lifetime. Embrace the discovery process with Him!

Bibliography & Suggested Readings

Defeating Dark Angels by Charles H. Kraft
The Three Battlegrounds by Francis Frangipane
Listening Prayer by Dave and Linda Olson
Hearing God by Dallas Willard
By My Authority by Charles H. Kraft
Healing Presence by Leanne Payne
Restoring the Christian Soul by Leanne Payne

Embracing Life Ministries Resources
Published by Xulon Press and available online

Embracing Life Series (ELS) A 14-session healing discipleship series for persons with life-altering conditions of all kinds.

Breaking Free... from the spirit of death (first edition) The text from which the current ***Guidebook Edition*** was derived.

More Glory! God's Healing Voice for Shame and Self-hatred This booklet for individual or group use offers real hope for Christians struggling with shame and self hatred.

More Hope! A Guide for Women Emerging... from the Shadow of Breast Cancer Reading, reflection and prayer for women struggling with issues related to breast cancer.

Other Resources
Damascus Road **(DVD)** A TBN produced interview with Jonathan Hunter featuring his testimony. Available at *www. embracinglife.us*.

www.EmbracingLife.us

All ELM resources are available on our website.

Please visit us for ministry updates on conferences, trainings, groups, and additional resources

Lightning Source UK Ltd.
Milton Keynes UK
UKHW02f0706161217
314561UK00005B/190/P